A BABY WITCHES GUIDE TO GREATNESS

By: Ascher Alchier

Dedication

This book is dedicated to the Matriarch of Moonlight, the weaver of white magic that drifts like mist through the tapestry of my lineage—my beloved grandmother. You bestowed upon us the legacy of the light, the gentle touch of the earth, the whisper of the wind, and the calmness of water. It was you who instilled the wisdom of balance, the courage to heal, and the strength to protect.

Your spirit, like an ever-present guardian, has marked each of us and every page of this journey. This book is etched with the essence of your teachings, reflecting the benevolence of your heart and the purity of your intentions. You walked the path so that we may dance in the moon's glow, grounded in the power you have passed through our bloodlines.

To the bright souls of my children and grandchildren, saplings ascending toward the sky's embrace—you are the dawn after the darkest night. May you grow firm in your roots yet graceful in your reach, illuminating the world with the radiant glow of understanding, love, and peaceful magic.

Within these pages lies more than knowledge; here is the legacy of our ancestors, the whisper of the forest, and the song of the stars, all waiting for you to unfold them with the same tenderness with which they were given. Grow, my dearest ones, in the light of your own truths, guided by the wisdom of the past and the brilliance of your own spirits. Shine, so that your light may join the chorus of the cosmos and continue the legacy of the white craft that sings through our veins.

With all the love that shines from the moon.

Table of Contents

Chapter 1 Introduction 1

Chapter 2 Understanding the Basics 3

Chapter 3 Setting up Your Altar and Sacred Space 8

Chapter 4 Embracing of Ethics 11

Chapter 5 Spell craft and Ritual Practice 15

Chapter 6 Connecting with Divination and Spirituality 17

Chapter 7 Embracing Nature's Wisdom and Herbal Magic 20

Chapter 8 Living in Alignment 24

Chapter 9 Crystals and uses 27

Chapter 10 Herbs and uses 36

Chapter 11 An Introduction to Runes 45

Chapter 12 Basic spell work for beginners 61

Chapter 1

Introduction

Welcome to the enchanting world of white witchcraft! This guide is your ultimate companion for mastering and embracing the ways of the white craft. Whether you're a curious novice or a seeker of knowledge, this book will equip you with the fundamental principles, rituals, and moral code.

The craft is a spiritual journey that embraces the natural order, emphasizes the balancing of energy, and promotes the well-being of oneself and others. As a white witch, you will learn to work with the elements of nature, tap into the universal power, and cultivate positive energy to bring harmony to your life and the world.

The craft is a practice that focuses on harnessing natural elements and energies benevolently and harmoniously. It is often associated with healing, protection, and aiding others. The term "white" is used to distinguish it from "black" or malevolent witchcraft, which is associated with malicious or negative intentions.

The natural elements hold a significant role in white witchcraft. The craft is deeply rooted in the five elements: Earth, Air, Fire, Water, and Spirit. These elements hold great significance in this practice, as they are believed to possess unique energies and symbolism that can be harnessed for magical purposes.

For example, Earth is associated with stability and the physical realm, making it an essential element in rituals related to prosperity and abundance. Similarly, Air is linked to communication and intellect, making it a powerful element to incorporate in rituals for clarity and inspiration. Fire represents passion and transformation, while Water is connected to emotions and intuition. These elements are often utilized in rituals for courage, emotional balance, and psychic awareness.

In addition to the elements, the craft also emphasizes aligning oneself with the natural rhythms and energies of the universe. This can be achieved through various practices such as meditation, visualization, and honoring the cycles of the moon and seasons. By doing so, practitioners seek to enhance their magical workings and spiritual growth.

Another important aspect of white witchcraft is the cultivation and manipulation of energy. This involves gathering, directing, and focusing energy for various purposes, which can be achieved through meditation and working with natural tools such as crystals and herbs. By honing their ability to sense and manipulate energy, practitioners can amplify the effectiveness of their spells and rituals.

Ultimately, white witchcraft is a diverse and personal spiritual practice that seeks to promote harmony with nature and work in alignment with the greater forces of the universe.

Chapter 2
Understanding the Basics

This chapter delves into the fundamental principles of the craft, where we will explore the core beliefs and practices. You will gain insight into the forces of nature, the cyclical nature of time, known as the Wheel of the Year, and the divine energies, all integral to the white crafter.

The Forces of Nature: White craft acknowledges the potency of the natural elements. Each element holds its distinct energy and symbolism, and white crafters often tap into their power to achieve balance and harmony in their lives.

Exploring Earth Magic: The element of Earth holds great significance and symbolism in the craft. It embodies stability, grounding, and the physical world while also representing abundance, nurturing, and a strong connection to nature. Crafters harness the Earth's energy in various rituals, spells, and meditative practices.

Some key aspects of the Earth element to practitioners:

- **Symbolism and Characteristics:** Earth is often linked to nurturing qualities, resilience, fertility, and material wealth. It serves as the strong foundation upon which life and existence thrive. In the craft, practitioners deeply honor and revere the Earth as a living, breathing entity, recognizing its vital role in sustaining life and providing essential resources.

- **Rituals and Enchantment:** The Earth element plays a crucial role in craft rituals and magical workings. This may involve utilizing natural elements like soil, stones, or plants in spell work, setting up altars adorned with Earth representations, and conducting ceremonies that honor the ever-changing seasons and cycles of nature.

Nature-Oriented Rituals: Host meaningful rituals and ceremonies that celebrate and pay homage to the natural world. Consider performing outdoor ceremonies, such as full moon or seasonal celebrations, in natural settings like forests, parks, or near bodies of water. Before and after these rituals, express gratitude to the Earth and consider participating in activities like litter clean-up or tree planting.

Tips for Sustainable Spell Work: Incorporate eco-friendly and sustainable materials into your spells and rituals. Use ingredients that are locally sourced, ethically harvested, or grown with minimal impact on the environment. For instance, opt for organic herbs, sustainably harvested resins, and environmentally friendly candles.

Nature meditation and grounding can be enhanced by regularly spending time in natural surroundings, allowing the Earth's energy to infuse and revitalize your spiritual practice. Engage in outdoor grounding and meditation. Walking meditations in nature will help you connect with the Earth's rhythms. Incorporating conservation efforts into your spiritual service can deepen your connection to the environment and contribute to saving our planet. Participate in community clean-up projects, support local conservation groups, and advocate for environmentally conscious policies.

To extend your spiritual path, make sustainable living practices a part of your daily life. This may include reducing energy consumption, minimizing waste, supporting ethical and eco-friendly businesses, and making choices that align with the values of environmental stewardship. Consider incorporating practices like composting, reducing single-use plastics, and supporting local and sustainable food sources. Develop a closer relationship with plants and herbs by learning about sustainable gardening, ethical wildcrafting, and herbal practices that align with ecological principles. Practice ethical harvesting, support native plant species, and consider growing magical herbs and plants using sustainable methods.

Spread your message of environmental stewardship within your community by sharing your knowledge and passion. Offer workshops, discussions, or educational events to highlight the connection between spirituality and environmentalism. Encourage others to join your efforts to protect the natural world, fostering a sense of collective responsibility and a shared connection to the Earth. By incorporating environmental stewardship into your spiritual practice, you can embody the principles of the craft in a tangible and impactful way. Remember that even small acts of environmental consciousness can contribute to the well-being of the Earth, and your dedication to sustainable spirituality can inspire others to join in the effort to protect and honor our shared environment.

Connecting with the Earth's Energy: A Guide to Grounding and Centering

Earth is often revered for its grounding properties, and those practicing craftwork often seek to align themselves with its stabilizing energy. Grounding practices are vital for cultivating a sense of inner stability and balance, allowing practitioners to feel more present in the moment. This connection with the Earth is believed to enhance mental clarity, emotional resilience, and overall spiritual well-being.

Grounding in magic involves immersing oneself in the Earth's energy, finding a centered state, and releasing any excess energy or distractions. By grounding, practitioners can establish a sense of equilibrium, essential for effective spellcasting, ritual work, and spiritual growth. By embodying these principles, practitioners can ground themselves in the Earth's energy in a tangible and impactful way. Every small act of environmental consciousness contributes to the well-being of the Earth's future.

When we dedicate ourselves to sustainable spirituality, we honor and protect our shared environment, inspiring others to join the effort. This collective commitment creates a ripple effect, leading to a more significant impact on the Earth's well-being. By grounding ourselves in the Earth's energy, we can cultivate a deeper connection with nature and become more attuned to its needs.

Grounding in magic goes beyond just connecting with the Earth's energy for personal benefit. It allows practitioners to tap into natural energy and flow it through their being, enhancing their magical abilities. This amplification of energy flow can bring a sense of balance to a practitioner, allowing for clarity and intention in their magical workings. Grounding also serves as a form of stress relief, alleviating feelings of anxiety, stress, or being overwhelmed.

By grounding, we can anchor our intentions in the physical realm, making our magical work more tangible and powerful. Grounding is a fundamental and essential aspect of magical workings. In today's fast-paced world, it's easy to become overwhelmed by anxiety and stress. However, by reconnecting with the stabilizing energy of the Earth, practitioners can find a sense of calm and balance. Additionally, mindful breathing exercises can aid in grounding by allowing you to fully inhabit the present moment and release any excess or disharmonious energy.

Incorporating physical activities such as yoga, qigong, or tai chi into your daily routine can also promote grounding. These practices cultivate a strong and stable energy flow within the body, helping to center and stabilize your energy. Utilizing grounding crystals like hematite, black tourmaline, or red jasper can also aid in centering and stabilizing your energy. Finally, through visualization and guided grounding meditations, you can deepen your connection with the Earth's energy and release any distractions or tensions, allowing the stabilizing force of the Earth to envelop you.

Incorporating Earth-Based Rituals

Design rituals specifically aimed at incorporating the grounding element, such as connecting barefoot with the Earth, indulging in a ceremonial grounding bath using natural salts and herbs, or constructing a sacred grounding altar to honor the Earth's energy. Integrating grounding into your magical practice can amplify the power of your spells, enhance your ritual performance, and nurture your spiritual growth. By establishing a profound connection with the Earth and mastering the art of grounding your energy, you can cultivate stability, clarity, and a heightened sense of presence in your magical workings. These foundational practices serve as a crucial aspect of honing your magical abilities and fostering a harmonious relationship with the natural world.

Herbalism and Plant Alchemy

Alchemists often develop a deep reverence for herbalism and plant magic as a means of working with the Earth's energy, harnessing the potency of herbs and plants in their spells, teas, incense, and healing concoctions.

Chapter 3
Setting up Your Altar and Sacred Space

Your altar or sacred spaces are physical locations and powerful tools for your spiritual practice. These spaces not only serve as a reminder of your connection to the divine but can also help you tap into your inner strength and intuition.

Choosing a Location:

Select a space that feels conducive to your magical practice. This could be a dedicated area in your home, such as a table, shelf, or corner of a room, where you can set up your altar and perform spell work undisturbed. Consider the energy of the space and the vibes it gives off. Look for a location that feels peaceful, harmonious, and aligned with your intentions for magical work. Some practitioners prefer to place their altar near a window, in a garden, or in a room with natural light to enhance the energy and connection to nature.

Creating the Altar:

Start by choosing a surface for your altar, such as a table, shelf, or cloth-covered surface. You may want to consider the size and shape of the surface based on the objects and tools you plan to include. As you set up your altar, consider the elements: Earth, Air, Fire, Water, and Spirit. Many practitioners choose to incorporate symbols or representations of these elements on their altars to establish a connection to the natural world and the sacred. This can also help create a balanced and harmonious energy in your sacred space.

Maintaining the Space:

Regularly cleanse and purify your altar and sacred space to keep the energy flowing. This can be done through practices such as smudging with sage, sprinkling salt, or using other cleansing rituals to remove any stagnant or unwanted energies. In addition to physical cleaning, it is also important to keep your altar and sacred space organized and clutter-free. This will help avoid distractions during your practice and maintain a clear and focused energy.

Remember to refresh the energy of your sacred space through meditation, visualization, and the intentional use of sound, such as chimes, bells, or singing bowls. This will help keep your space in alignment with your intentions and enhance the effectiveness of your magical practice.

Invoking Intention:

Consecrate your altar and sacred space with intention. You can perform a ritual to dedicate the space to your magical work and invite the support of energies or deities that resonate with your practice. This is a powerful way to infuse your space with purpose and align it with your intentions.

As you consecrate your space, you are also creating a boundary between the mundane and the spiritual, allowing you to focus and connect with the energies you wish to work with. Set and renew your intentions for the altar and sacred space. Consider the purpose of your spell work, the energies you wish to cultivate, and the qualities you seek to invite into your space. This can be done through visualization, prayer, or meditation. By regularly renewing your intentions, you reaffirm your commitment to your practice and create a clear intention for the energy you wish to manifest in your space.

Incorporating Tools and Symbols:

Choose tools and symbols that are meaningful to your practice. These could include a cauldron, athame (ritual dagger), wand, chalice, tarot cards, runes, herbs, and other items that align with your magical work. These tools and symbols can serve as physical representations of your intentions and help amplify the energy in your space. As you select and place these items on your altar, you are infusing them with your personal energy and intention.

Adapting to Change:

Be open to adapting and evolving your sacred space over time. As your practice grows and changes, you may find that the items, symbols, and energies on your altar need to be adjusted to reflect your current path and intentions. Your sacred space is a reflection of your inner world, and as you evolve and grow, so too will your space. Trust your intuition and allow your sacred space to evolve with you.

Remember, there is no right or wrong way to create and maintain a sacred space. It is a deeply personal and individual journey, and the most important thing is to listen to your intuition and follow your heart. As you work with your altar, stay attuned to the energy and intention you have set, and allow your sacred space to support and guide you on your spiritual path.

Chapter 4
Embracing of Ethics

The craft is a practice rooted in compassion and kindness toward others. This is reflected in the ethical guidelines that practitioners follow, serving as a moral compass for their actions and intentions. These guidelines emphasize the importance of using magic for the greater good and avoiding harm to others. Crafters believe that their magic should bring positive change and healing to themselves and the world around them. One of the key principles of the craft is the belief in the interconnectedness of all things.

Practitioners see themselves as part of a larger whole and recognize the impact of their actions on others and the environment. This perspective encourages them to act with empathy, respect, and responsibility toward all beings. It also guides them to use their magic responsibly and conscientiously, understanding that every spell and ritual has consequences that can ripple beyond their immediate intentions.

In addition to their focus on ethical practices, white witches have a deep reverence for nature and the cycles of the earth. They believe that magic is a natural force that can be harnessed and amplified through rituals and spells. As such, they strive to live in harmony with nature and use their magic to protect and heal the earth. This connection to the natural world is an integral part of the craft path and serves as a source of inspiration and guidance for their practices.

Practitioners understand the interconnectedness of all living beings and the environment, believing that every action, no matter how small, has a ripple effect on the world around them. This awareness of the delicate balance of nature guides them in their pursuit of "harm none." By being mindful of their words, thoughts, and actions, practitioners aim to create a positive and harmonious energy that benefits not only themselves but also those around them.

The concept of "harm none" also extends to the use of magic. Practitioners believe that magic is a powerful force that should be used responsibly and with good intentions. They carefully consider the potential consequences of their spells and take precautions to prevent any harm from affecting others or the environment. This mindful approach to magic sets white craft apart from other forms of witchcraft and reinforces practitioners' dedication to living in harmony with nature.

In essence, white craft is a way of life that revolves around promoting peace, compassion, and harmony. By adhering to the principle of "harm none," white witches aim to create a better world for themselves and those around them. This dedication to ethical living and alignment with nature makes white witchcraft a truly unique and powerful spiritual path.

White crafters also prioritize respecting the free will of others in their practice. This includes refraining from using magic to control others and respecting their choices and decisions. By promoting the value of free will, practitioners aim to create a world where individuals can make their own choices without fear of outside influence. This dedication to respecting free will goes hand in hand with the principle of "harm none" in the craft. By choosing to respect others' autonomy, they foster harmony and promote peace within their communities.

This emphasis on consent and ethical considerations sets white witchcraft apart from other spiritual paths, making it a unique and powerful practice that values the well-being and agency of all individuals. Practitioners must carefully consider the potential consequences of their actions and ensure they align with their ethical code. By harnessing the power of positive intentions, they manifest their desires and create meaningful change in the world around them. This dedication to using magic for good distinguishes white witchcraft from other spiritual paths and contributes to its power.

Overall, white witchcraft is a path focused on promoting love, compassion, and peace in the world. Through the use of positive intentions and ethical principles, practitioners harness the power of magic to create positive change and live in harmony with others. By staying true to their beliefs and values, white witches make a meaningful impact on the world and contribute to a more compassionate and peaceful society.

By taking personal responsibility, white witches not only harness the power of magic but also understand the importance of using it for good. They are conscious of the potential consequences of their actions and strive to create positive change in the world. This mindset is deeply rooted in their beliefs and values, as they seek to live in harmony with others and the environment. Through their magic, white witches heal, protect, and bring balance to the world. By staying true to their beliefs, they inspire others to do the same.

Their actions are guided by a strong sense of personal responsibility, and they recognize that their magical abilities come with great responsibility. For white witches, personal responsibility extends beyond their magical work to all aspects of their lives, including their relationships and environmental impact. They strive to live in alignment with their values, taking ownership of their actions and being accountable for their influence on the world. By doing so, they not only create positive change but also set an example for others to follow.

Practitioners view themselves as interconnected with the environment and strive to live in harmony with nature. This connection is reflected in their actions, as they seek to maintain a respectful relationship with the natural world. They understand the importance of sustainable practices and minimizing harm to the environment. As stewards of the earth, they work to protect and nurture its balance.

In addition to their ethical responsibilities, white crafters draw spiritual power from nature. They find inspiration and energy in the cycles of the natural world, such as the changing seasons and the phases of the moon. This connection helps them gain a deeper understanding of the world around them and guides their actions toward positive change.

By fostering a deep connection with nature and living in harmony with it, white witches not only create positive change in the world but also set an example for others. This includes practicing magic with intention, seeking consent from all involved, and always acting with compassion and kindness. By aligning their actions with these principles, practitioners strive to bring balance and harmony to their surroundings.

Ultimately, the practice of witchcraft is a deeply personal and evolving journey. Whether one identifies as a white witch or not, it is important to approach the practice with an open mind and a willingness to continually learn and grow. By doing so, we can all strive to be examples for others in respecting and protecting the natural world.

Chapter 5
Spell craft and Ritual Practice

Now, we will explore the practice of spellcraft and ritual work. Spellcraft, also known as magic, involves harnessing the natural energies of the universe to create positive change in one's life. By understanding the fundamental principles and practices of spellcraft, one can learn to use their energy and intention to achieve their goals.

One of the key concepts of spellcraft is the importance of intention. It is crucial to have a clearly defined and well-intentioned desire or goal in mind when performing a spell. Without a strong intent, the energy behind the spell may be weakened, making it less effective. This is why it is essential to fully understand what you want to achieve and why before embarking on any spell work.

Another essential component of spellcraft is energy. Practitioners often use various methods to raise, direct, and project energy to fuel their spells. This can be achieved through visualization, meditation, chanting, or other techniques. By manipulating and directing energy, one can achieve their desired outcome and manifest their intentions into reality. However, it is essential to remember that energy is a powerful force and should always be used responsibly and with ethical considerations.

Ethical Considerations

Many practitioners of spellcraft adhere to ethical principles that guide their magical practices. These may include the Wiccan Rede, which states,

"An it harm none, do what ye will," emphasizing the responsibility to ensure that one's actions do not cause harm to others. This code of ethics also encourages practitioners to take responsibility for their actions and the consequences of their spells. It reminds them to use their powers responsibly and with good intentions, as energy is a powerful force that can have lasting effects on the world around us.

Respect for the free will of others is a foundational ethical consideration in spellcraft. Practitioners generally avoid attempting to influence or control others without their consent. This principle highlights the importance of respecting individual autonomy and personal boundaries. It also emphasizes the need for clear communication and consent in any magical workings that involve other people. By following this principle, spellcraft practitioners aim to create a harmonious and balanced relationship with those around them.

Positive intentions are encouraged in spellcraft. Practitioners often focus on casting spells that promote well-being, personal growth, and harmony, both for themselves and others. This is because the energy that we put out into the universe often comes back to us in some form. By focusing on positive intentions, practitioners hope to attract positive outcomes and create a better world for themselves and others. This aligns with the idea that energy follows intention and reinforces the importance of responsible and ethical spellcraft or manifesting.

Chapter 6
Connecting with Divination and Spirituality

Practitioners often seek guidance and insight through divination tools and practices. In this chapter, you will discover methods of divination and explore ways to deepen your spiritual connection with the divine. These tools can be powerful aids in connecting with the spiritual realm and accessing intuitive insights and higher wisdom.

Using divination tools with intention and reverence is essential in fostering a deeper spiritual connection. Setting a clear and positive intention before a divination session helps align your conscious energy with the divine or intuitive realm. This intention shapes the energy and focus of the divination process, making it more effective and meaningful.

In addition to intention, honoring the divination tools themselves is crucial. These tools are not simply objects; they embody potent symbolism and spiritual significance. By treating them with respect and care—such as storing them in a dedicated space, cleansing them energetically, and handling them mindfully—you honor their spiritual energies and create a harmonious relationship with them. This deepens your connection with the tools and the spiritual realm they represent.

To further enhance the spiritual connection, creating a sacred space for divination practice can be beneficial. This may include setting up an altar with meaningful symbols, burning incense or candles, and engaging in grounding or centering rituals to invite higher vibrations into the space.

Incorporating rituals that align with your spiritual beliefs can intensify the divination experience and deepen your connection with the divine.

Finally, regular use and practice of divination tools can help individuals cultivate their intuition. These tools serve as mirrors that reflect and amplify intuitive insights. By trusting their inner guidance and actively engaging with the tools, individuals can strengthen their spiritual awareness and connection to the divine or universal consciousness. This can lead to a deeper understanding of oneself and the world around them.

Seeking Spiritual Guidance

Engaging in divination offers a channel for seeking spiritual guidance and wisdom. Whether consulting tarot cards, casting runes, or scrying, the process can provide valuable insights, confirmations, and perspectives that resonate with one's spiritual journey. Embracing the messages received with openness and discernment can foster spiritual growth and understanding.

Reflection and Integration

After a divination session, take time to reflect on the messages, symbols, and intuitive impressions received. Journaling or meditating on the insights gained can facilitate deeper integration with one's spiritual path and assist in applying the guidance to practical situations or inner transformation. This reflective process allows individuals to fully process and internalize the messages received, leading to a more comprehensive understanding of themselves and their place in the world.

The connection between divination and spirituality is a deeply personal and dynamic journey that evolves over time. Through consistent practice, reverence, and genuine engagement with divination tools, individuals can develop a profound communion with their spiritual essence, expand their intuitive capacities, and align with the guiding forces of the universe. By trusting their inner guidance and actively engaging with the tools, individuals can strengthen their spiritual awareness and connection to the divine or universal consciousness. This allows for a deeper understanding of oneself and the world around them, ultimately leading to a more fulfilling and purposeful life.

Chapter 7
Embracing Nature's Wisdom and Herbal Magic

The practice of white witchcraft is deeply rooted in nature and its many gifts. As you delve deeper into these chapters, you will discover the power of using herbs, plants, and the wisdom of the natural world in your magical practice. Herbal magic is a fundamental aspect of craft work, utilizing the healing and magical properties of plants in spell work, rituals, and everyday life.

By creating herbal remedies, sachets, and charms, practitioners can enhance their intentions and strengthen their connection to the mystical energies of nature. In addition to herbal magic, embracing nature's wisdom is also a crucial element in craft work. By spending time in nature and observing the cycles of the seasons, practitioners can attune themselves to the natural world and gain insight, inspiration, and a deep appreciation for the interconnectedness of all living things.

To fully embrace nature's wisdom and herbal magic, it is important to recognize and revere the spiritual and healing energies found in the natural world. This involves developing a deep connection to nature, respecting the spirits of plants, and approaching them with reverence and gratitude. By following these key principles, practitioners can tap into the powerful energies of nature and enhance their magical practice.

Herbal magic is a practice that deeply connects individuals with the natural world. It involves understanding and respecting the spirits and energies of plants and utilizing them in spells and rituals. The use of herbs in magic aligns with the elemental energies of earth, air, fire, and water, and practitioners carefully consider these correspondences when selecting ingredients for their spells.

Intention plays a vital role in herbal magic, as practitioners choose specific herbs and plants based on their correspondences and healing properties. By intentionally selecting ingredients, the potency of spells and rituals is enhanced. This allows for a deeper connection to the natural world and its powerful energies.

A Herbal Talisman for Protection and Harmony

This spell utilizes the energies of herbs such as rosemary for protection and lavender for harmony, along with the amplifying properties of a clear quartz crystal. By infusing these ingredients with a specific intention and creating a talisman to carry with them, practitioners can align themselves with the healing energies of the earth and manifest their desires for protection and harmony in their lives.

Creating a talisman is a powerful way for practitioners to connect with the healing energies of the earth and manifest their desires. By carefully selecting and combining herbs and other natural materials, this sachet serves as a physical representation of the intention for peace and relaxation. By carrying this sachet with them, practitioners can align themselves with the calming energies of lavender, chamomile, and mint, inviting peace and relaxation into their lives.

Similarly, this protection charm utilizes the power of natural materials to create a sense of safety and security in the home. By combining a clear quartz crystal and dried rosemary, this charm creates a protective barrier around the home. As the practitioner holds the charm and envisions a glowing light surrounding their home, they reinforce their intention for protection and safety. By hanging the charm near the entrance of the home or in a prominent place, it serves as a constant reminder of the protective energies at work. By periodically recharging the charm, the practitioner can continue to benefit from its protective properties. This charm is a perfect example of the power of intention and the use of natural materials in creating a talisman for protection.

A Healing Talisman

This spell utilizes the energies of herbs, allowing practitioners to continue benefiting from their supportive properties. The combination of eucalyptus and peppermint leaves creates a powerful blend that can aid in clearing congestion and promoting respiratory health. Using natural materials such as herbs and crystals is a perfect example of the power of intention in creating a talisman for healing.

The act of creating this remedy with the intention of supporting respiratory health adds an extra layer of healing energy to the steam. As we inhale the aromatic vapors, we can focus on the cleansing and opening of our airways, allowing the natural properties of the herbs to work their magic.

It's important to remember that these herbal remedies are not a substitute for professional medical advice. Be aware of any potential allergies and consult a doctor if you have any underlying health conditions or are pregnant. With that in mind, incorporating herbal remedies into self-care routines can be a powerful way to enhance well-being. The next time you need respiratory support, try creating this herbal talisman with steam and harness the healing energies of nature.

Nature has a powerful ability to heal and support our well-being. This herbal steam harnesses the healing energies of nature and is a simple yet effective way to enhance overall health.

Attuning to Nature

Attuning to nature involves developing a deep connection and harmonious relationship with the natural world. To achieve this, spend time outdoors and engage in regular activities such as walking or hiking. Practice mindfulness by being aware of your surroundings and cultivating a habit of mindful breathing and grounding exercises.

It is also beneficial to learn about the natural world and participate in earth-centered rituals such as meditation or yoga outdoors. Communing with plants and trees is another way to establish a deeper connection with nature. Take the opportunity to touch, smell, and feel their energy, engaging in practices such as tree hugging or sitting in quiet contemplation. If possible, cultivate a garden or tend to indoor plants to foster a sense of reciprocity and appreciation for the life force inherent in nature.

Additionally, observing solar and lunar cycles and participating in conservation efforts can strengthen our connection to the earth and its delicate balance. These practices help quiet the mind and increase our ability to connect with the present moment, allowing for a deeper appreciation of the beauty and vitality of nature.

Nurturing an Attitude of Gratitude

Take a moment to express gratitude for the earth and all its gifts, recognizing the abundance and interconnectedness of all living beings. This shift in perspective—from one of consumption to one of stewardship—fosters a deeper sense of reciprocity and respect for the environment.

Through these intentional practices, we can cultivate a deep connection with the earth and its delicate balance. This connection can lead to a heightened sense of responsibility toward the natural world and a desire to participate in conservation efforts.

Ultimately, by fostering a sense of harmony and interconnectedness with nature, we can cultivate a more peaceful and sustainable world for all beings.

Chapter 8

Living in Alignment

Now we will explore ways to integrate practices into your daily life and embrace guiding principles for personal growth and positive impact. One of the key ways to do this is through the practice of mindfulness and gratitude. By incorporating these principles into your daily routine, you can deepen your connection to the natural world and align yourself with the positive energies of white witchcraft.

Mindfulness and gratitude are not just important for magical work but also for overall well-being and happiness. By being mindful, you bring your focus to the present moment and become more aware of your surroundings. This can help you appreciate the beauty and abundance that surrounds you, leading to a greater sense of gratitude. When you cultivate gratitude, you attract more positive energies and experiences into your life.

Another way to integrate mindfulness and gratitude into your magical practice is through grounding and centering techniques. These practices involve connecting with the Earth's energy, focusing on the breath, and finding balance within oneself. By doing so, you become more present and grounded, which is essential for effective magical work. Grounding and centering also help you to be more mindful of your intentions and actions, allowing for more intentional and powerful magic. So, remember to take a few moments to ground and center before engaging in any magical work.

Grounding and centering can also be incorporated into daily activities, such as taking a walk in nature or practicing yoga. These practices not only help to connect with the Earth but also allow for moments of stillness and reflection. By slowing down and being present, one can notice the small details and beauty in everyday life, which can bring a sense of peace and grounding.

A key aspect of grounding and centering is connecting with one's own energy and inner self. This can be done through meditation, visualization, or simply taking a few deep breaths. By tuning into one's own inner power and intuition, one can better align their intentions and actions with their magical work, resulting in a more potent and authentic practice.

In addition to its benefits for magical work, cultivating mindfulness through grounding and centering can also have positive effects on overall well-being. By being present and grounded in the moment, one can reduce stress and anxiety, improve focus and clarity, and increase self-awareness. So, while these practices are essential for effective magic, they can also bring about personal growth and a deeper connection with oneself and the world around us.

As magical practitioners, we understand the importance of being present and grounded in the moment. By incorporating mindfulness into our magical practices, we not only enhance our abilities to cast effective spells but also experience personal growth.

Through offering rituals, we can express gratitude and deepen our connection with the spiritual beings, deities, or natural world we work with. By engaging in these rituals mindfully, we show our appreciation and respect for the gifts we receive.

In addition to offering rituals, mindfulness can also be applied to the actual act of spell casting. By approaching our magical work with intention, focus, and awareness, we can cultivate a deeper sense of mindfulness and intention behind our spells. This may involve incorporating meditation, visualization, and breathwork into our spell casting to heighten our concentration and intention. By aligning our thoughts, words, and actions with the desired outcome, we can enhance the effectiveness of our spells and deepen our connection with the magical energies we work with.

Our connection to the sacred is a vital part of our spiritual journey. By staying true to our intentions and aligning our thoughts, words, and actions with the universe, we can create a powerful and meaningful practice of magic. Let us continue to honor and nurture our sacred spaces, and in doing so, honor and nurture our own spiritual growth.

Chapter 9

Crystals and uses

There are countless crystals used in magic, each with its unique properties and associations. Amethyst is a beautiful crystal that has been used for centuries for its calming and protective properties. It is believed to have the ability to relieve stress and promote inner peace, making it a popular choice for those seeking emotional and mental balance.

In addition to its calming effects, amethyst is also known for its ability to aid in spiritual growth and enhance intuition. This makes it a valuable tool for those looking to deepen their spiritual practices and connect with their inner selves. One of the most interesting aspects of amethyst is its ability to enhance the properties of other crystals. When used in combination with other stones, it can amplify their energies and make them more effective. This makes it a valuable asset for those who work with multiple crystals in their magical practices.

Amethyst is also believed to protect against negative energy and promote overall physical and emotional well-being. This makes it a must-have for anyone looking to create a peaceful and harmonious environment. Whether used alone or in combination with other crystals, amethyst is a staple in many magical practices. Its calming and protective properties, as well as its ability to enhance intuition and promote spiritual growth, make it a valuable addition to any collection. So, the next time you're feeling stressed or overwhelmed, reach for your amethyst and let its soothing energy bring you back to a state of peace and balance.

Clear Quartz is a powerful and versatile crystal that has been used for centuries for its healing properties. It is known as the "master healer" because of its ability to amplify the energy of other crystals and promote balance and harmony within the body. Its clear and transparent appearance symbolizes clarity and focus, making it a popular choice for those seeking mental and emotional stability.

In addition to its physical healing properties, clear quartz is also believed to enhance intuition and promote spiritual growth. Its high vibrational energy can help open the mind and facilitate a deeper connection with oneself and the universe. This makes it a valuable addition to any crystal collection, especially for those on a spiritual journey or seeking inner peace. Next time you're feeling stressed or overwhelmed, reach for your clear quartz and allow its soothing energy to bring you back to a state of peace and balance. Whether used on its own or in combination with other crystals, clear quartz is a powerful tool for promoting physical, mental, and spiritual well-being. Its versatility and healing abilities make it a must-have for anyone looking to enhance their overall health and wellness.

Rose Quartz is an essential crystal for matters of the heart and emotional well-being. Its soft pink hue symbolizes love, compassion, and nurturing, making it a popular choice for those seeking to heal and strengthen their relationships. This crystal is also known for promoting self-love and attracting love into one's life, making it an important tool for enhancing overall emotional balance.

Whether used in jewelry, placed in your home or workspace, or carried on your person, rose quartz can bring a sense of tranquility and comfort. Its loving energy can help soothe the heart and mind, allowing for a state of peace and balance to be achieved. Combining rose quartz with other crystals, such as clear quartz, can amplify its healing properties and bring a deeper sense of harmony to one's life.

In addition to its emotional benefits, rose quartz is also believed to have physical healing properties. It is said to promote circulation, improve skin health, and aid in ailments related to the heart, lungs, and kidneys. This versatile crystal is a must-have for anyone looking to enhance their overall health and well-being, both physically and emotionally. Incorporating rose quartz into your daily routine can bring a sense of calm and positivity, helping you to live a more balanced and fulfilling life.

Black Tourmaline is a versatile crystal that can help protect against negative energy and promote feelings of security and stability. It is often used as a barrier against harmful influences, making it an essential addition to anyone's collection. When used in combination with rose quartz, it can create a powerful force to enhance overall health and well-being.

Incorporating Black Tourmaline into your daily routine can help bring balance and positivity to your life. By creating a protective barrier, it allows you to let go of any negative energy that may be holding you back and focus on living a more fulfilling life. This crystal is also known for its ability to ground and center your energy, allowing you to feel more connected to yourself and your surroundings. With its calming and protective properties, Black Tourmaline is a must-have for anyone looking to improve their well-being.

Citrine is a powerful crystal that radiates an optimistic and joyful energy. Its bright and sunny appearance makes it perfect for attracting abundance and prosperity into your life. This crystal is also known for its ability to bring about positive changes and manifest your desires into reality. Whether you are looking to improve your career, relationships, or overall well-being, Citrine can help you achieve your goals.

Not only is Citrine a magnet for prosperity and success, but it also has a strong connection to the solar plexus chakra. This chakra is responsible for confidence, self-esteem, and personal power. By working with Citrine, you can tap into this energy center and boost your self-confidence, allowing you to take risks and pursue your dreams with courage and determination.

In addition to its manifestation properties, Citrine is also a great crystal for promoting joy and happiness in your life. Its vibrant energy can help you let go of negative thoughts and emotions, allowing you to embrace a more positive outlook. By incorporating Citrine into your daily life, you can experience a more fulfilling and joyful existence, filled with abundance and prosperity.

Selenite is a powerful crystal that can bring positive energy into your life. Its soothing vibrations can help you release stress and tension, allowing you to feel more at peace. By incorporating Selenite into your daily routine, you can create a sense of balance and harmony within yourself.

Not only does Selenite have physical benefits, but it also has spiritual benefits. It is believed to open up the crown chakra and enhance spiritual awareness and intuition. This can help you connect with your inner self and gain a deeper understanding of your emotions and thoughts. Selenite can also aid in meditation and promote a sense of inner peace and tranquility.

Incorporating Selenite into your daily life can have a profound impact on your overall well-being. Its cleansing and purifying properties can help release negative energy and promote joy and happiness. With its ability to bring balance to the mind, body, and spirit, Selenite is a powerful crystal to have in your collection. So, take some time to connect with this crystal and experience its transformative effects for yourself.

The ancient Egyptians believed that Lapis Lazuli had the power to connect one's physical self with their spiritual self, making it a highly sought-after stone for spiritual growth and development. Its deep blue color is said to symbolize the vastness of the universe and the wisdom that can be gained through self-reflection and inner vision. This makes it a valuable crystal for those seeking to expand their consciousness and deepen their understanding of the world around them.

In addition to its spiritual properties, Lapis Lazuli is also known for its ability to improve communication and enhance relationships. It can help release negative energy and promote harmony and understanding between individuals. This is especially useful for those who struggle with expressing themselves or understanding the perspectives of others. By working with this crystal, one can gain a greater sense of clarity and empathy, leading to more fulfilling and meaningful connections with others.

Lapis Lazuli is a powerful crystal that offers a multitude of benefits for the mind, body, and spirit. Its transformative effects can bring balance to all aspects of one's life, creating a sense of joy and happiness. By taking the time to connect with this crystal, one can tap into its vast potential and experience positive changes in their life. Whether seeking spiritual growth, improved communication, or a deeper understanding of oneself, Lapis Lazuli is a valuable tool for anyone looking to enhance their well-being and live a more fulfilling life.

Peridot is a beautiful crystal that has been used for centuries to help individuals connect with their inner power and potential. This gorgeous green gemstone is known for its ability to promote growth and renewal, making it a valuable tool for those seeking positive changes in their lives. With its vibrant energy, Peridot is believed to attract abundance and prosperity, making it a must-have for anyone looking to enhance their financial situation.

But Peridot's benefits go beyond material wealth. This crystal is also highly regarded for its ability to promote personal growth and transformation. By tapping into its energy, one can experience a deep sense of renewal and rejuvenation, helping them to shed old habits and patterns that no longer serve them. This makes Peridot a valuable tool for those on a journey of self-discovery and personal development.

Whether you are seeking spiritual growth, improved communication, or a deeper understanding of yourself, Peridot is a powerful crystal that can help you achieve your goals. Its energy is known to enhance intuition and promote a positive outlook, making it a valuable companion for anyone looking to live a more fulfilling and meaningful life. With Peridot by your side, you can tap into your infinite potential and create positive changes in all areas of your life.

Tiger's Eye is a powerful stone that has long been revered for its protective qualities and its ability to promote courage and personal empowerment. This beautiful stone is known for its mesmerizing golden-brown color and its reflective, chatoyant surface, which is said to resemble the eye of a tiger. But beyond its physical beauty, Tiger's Eye is also known for its incredible energetic properties.

In addition to its protective qualities, Tiger's Eye is also known to enhance intuition and promote a positive outlook. This makes it a valuable companion for anyone looking to live a more fulfilling and meaningful life. With Tiger's Eye by your side, you can tap into your infinite potential and create positive changes in all areas of your life.

This stone is believed to boost confidence and dispel fear, allowing you to face challenges with courage and determination. Whether you are looking to overcome obstacles, find success in your career, or simply boost your confidence and live a more fulfilling life, Tiger's Eye is the perfect stone to have by your side. Its powerful energy can help you tap into your inner strength and wisdom, allowing you to make positive changes and reach your full potential. Keep this stone close to you and let its energy guide you on your journey towards a more empowered and fulfilling life.

Fluorite is also a popular protective stone that helps shield against negative energies and electromagnetic radiation. It can aid in balancing and aligning all the chakras, creating a sense of harmony and equilibrium in one's life. With its strong and vibrant energy, Fluorite increases intuition and spiritual awareness, making it a valuable tool for meditation and spiritual growth.

This crystal is also believed to have powerful healing properties, aiding in the treatment of both physical and emotional ailments. It is said to be beneficial for the respiratory system, helping to alleviate symptoms of asthma and other respiratory issues. Additionally, Fluorite is thought to help relieve stress and anxiety, promoting a sense of calm and relaxation.

By keeping Fluorite close, its energy can help clear mental fog and confusion, allowing for better decision-making and problem-solving. It can also provide stability and strength during challenging times, helping you tap into your inner wisdom and resilience. Embrace the power of Fluorite and let it guide you toward a more empowered and fulfilling life.

Moonstone is a powerful crystal that has been used for centuries to enhance feminine energy and intuition. Its soft and gentle energy promotes a deep connection with the cycles of the moon, fostering heightened spiritual awareness and a sense of inner peace. This crystal is perfect for anyone looking to tap into their intuition and enhance their psychic abilities.

The soothing energy of Moonstone can also help alleviate feelings of anxiety and stress. When used during meditation or placed under your pillow at night, it can promote restful sleep and assist in unlocking your inner wisdom. This can be especially beneficial during times of confusion, allowing for clearer decision-making and problem-solving.

As you connect with the lunar energies of Moonstone, you will also find a sense of stability and strength to guide you through life's challenges. Embracing the power of Moonstone can create a shift in your life toward empowerment and fulfillment. Its energy will guide you toward your true purpose and help you trust your instincts. Whether you seek a deeper spiritual connection or simply a sense of inner peace, Moonstone is a powerful crystal to support your journey. Allow its ethereal energy to envelop you and guide you toward a more aligned and fulfilling life.

Hematite is a powerful crystal that can help you tap into your inner strength and stability. Whether you are feeling overwhelmed or lost, this stone anchors you in the present moment and provides a sense of protection. Its energy helps dispel negative energies, allowing you to find peace and balance.

In addition to its grounding properties, Hematite is also known for its ability to promote courage and determination. It gives you the strength to face challenges and overcome obstacles in your life. This crystal is a helpful tool for those seeking to find their inner power and take control of their destiny. Its energy instills stability and confidence, guiding you toward a more aligned and fulfilling path.

As you journey toward a deeper spiritual connection, Hematite serves as a valuable companion. Its energy encourages you to release fears and doubts, trust your instincts, and follow your intuition. This crystal is a reminder that you have the power within you to create a life filled with peace, strength, and purpose. Allow Hematite to be your guide as you embark on a journey of self-discovery and growth.

Malachite is a powerful crystal that helps release negative patterns and emotions, allowing you to move forward with a clear mind and heart. Its vibrant green color symbolizes growth and transformation, making it a perfect companion for those seeking personal development and self-discovery. Holding this crystal, you can feel its energy flow through you, guiding you toward a more peaceful and fulfilling life.

This crystal is also known for its protective properties, shielding you from negative energies and influences. By creating a strong energetic barrier, Malachite instills confidence and strength, helping you trust your instincts and follow your intuition. It serves as a reminder that you have the power within you to create the life you desire—one filled with peace, strength, and purpose.

Allow Malachite to be your guide on your journey of self-discovery and healing. Its energy supports you every step of the way, helping you release old patterns and heal emotional wounds. With Malachite by your side, you can let go of the past and embrace a brighter future. Trust in its transformative power, and let it guide you toward a life of balance, joy, and fulfillment.

Carnelian is a crystal often used to boost energy and evoke passion and creativity. This vibrant stone encourages you to embrace your inner vitality and make the most of life. It is associated with courage and motivation, making it the perfect companion for taking on new challenges and ventures.

Beyond its ability to ignite motivation and drive, Carnelian is also known for its healing properties. It helps release old patterns and heal emotional wounds, allowing you to let go of the past and move forward with optimism. With Carnelian by your side, you can trust in its transformative power to guide you toward a life of balance, joy, and fulfillment. This crystal serves as a reminder to embrace your true self and live life to the fullest.

Aventurine is a crystal that has been cherished throughout history for its powerful properties. With its beautiful green color, it is known as a stone of opportunity and luck. This crystal is believed to attract prosperity and encourage a positive outlook on life. Its energy is often associated with abundance and good fortune, making it a popular choice for those seeking to manifest their desires.

The name Aventurine comes from the Italian phrase *a ventura*, meaning "by chance," reflecting its reputation as a lucky stone that brings unexpected opportunities and success. Aventurine is also believed to help release old patterns and habits, allowing for personal growth and transformation.

Its calming and soothing energy helps reduce stress and anxiety while promoting a sense of inner peace and balance. With Aventurine by your side, you can trust in its powerful energy to guide you toward a brighter and more fulfilling future. This crystal reminds you to embrace your true self, take chances, and step out of your comfort zone, opening up new opportunities and experiences.

Aventurine is a beautiful crystal that can bring abundance, luck, and joy into your life, making it a must-have for anyone seeking to create a more positive and prosperous future. When it comes to energy work, Aventurine is a popular choice due to its ability to attract abundance and joy. However, it's important to remember that this is just one of many crystals with unique energetic properties and associations.

Each crystal offers its own set of benefits, and it's crucial to tune into your intuition to find the ones that align with your intentions and needs. While crystals can enhance our energy and help manifest our desires, it's important to approach their use with mindfulness and respect. Setting clear intentions and working with crystals consciously ensures that we remain aligned with our highest good.

As we take chances and step out of our comfort zone, crystals like Aventurine can support us on our journey toward a more positive and prosperous future.

Chapter 10

Herbs and uses

Herbs have been a vital part of craft work for centuries, used for their magical properties and healing abilities. Each herb holds a unique energy and is associated with distinct intentions and purposes. Plants and herbs are seen as living beings with their own consciousness and spirit. In the practice of craft work, herbs are used in various ways, including burning, brewing, and carrying as talismans.

Aventurine, a crystal associated with prosperity and abundance, is often used alongside herbs to amplify their magical properties. Using herbs in combination with crystals not only enhances the effectiveness of the herbs but also ensures that one is working in alignment with their highest good. Let's delve deeper into the uses and benefits of herbs, providing a comprehensive guide for those looking to incorporate them into their practice. From protection to love spells, each herb has a specific purpose that can help in manifesting one's desires.

By taking chances and stepping out of one's comfort zone, herbs like lavender and rosemary can support the journey toward a more positive and prosperous future. With the right intentions and the support of herbs and crystals, one can tap into their inner power and manifest their dreams into reality. When embarking on a journey toward change, it's important to have the right tools and mindset. This is where herbs like rosemary come into play. With its purifying and protective properties, this herb can help clear the path for positive growth and manifestation. Not only does it cleanse spaces, but it also aids in mental clarity and memory, allowing one to focus on their intentions and dreams. Additionally, rosemary is often associated with love and remembrance, reminding us to hold onto our passions and never forget our goals.

Another herb that can support our journey of taking chances and stepping out of our comfort zone is lavender. Known for its calming and soothing properties, lavender can help ease any fears or anxieties that may arise during this process. It also promotes relaxation and balance, allowing for a clearer connection with our inner power. Lavender is also believed to attract abundance and prosperity, making it a great companion on the path toward a more positive and prosperous future. With the support of rosemary and lavender, one can tap into their full potential and manifest their dreams into reality.

Lavender has a long history of being used for its calming properties. Its soothing scent has been known to promote relaxation, reduce stress and anxiety, and alleviate insomnia. It's also believed to have the ability to attract love and happiness into one's life. In addition, lavender has been used for centuries in spiritual practices to connect with one's inner power and intuition.

The combination of rosemary and lavender makes for a powerful duo in manifesting dreams and attracting abundance. Rosemary is known for its ability to enhance memory and focus, while lavender promotes relaxation and peace. Together, they create a perfect balance of mental clarity and relaxation, allowing one to tap into their full potential and achieve their goals. Whether in a spiritual practice or daily life, this combination can help one stay focused and motivated on the path toward a positive and prosperous future. With the support of these two herbs, the possibilities are endless in manifesting one's desires into reality.

Sage is not just a powerful herb for cleansing; it also has the ability to enhance one's spiritual practice. Its calming and grounding properties make it a perfect accompaniment for meditation, helping to reach a deeper state of focus and clarity. Sage can also aid in connecting with one's intuition and inner wisdom, making it a valuable tool for self-discovery and growth. When combined with the motivational properties of rosemary, sage becomes even more potent in helping individuals achieve their goals.

Rosemary is known for its ability to increase mental clarity, memory, and concentration. This makes it a perfect complement to sage, as it can help one stay focused and motivated on their desired path, whether in daily life or their spiritual journey. By incorporating sage and rosemary into one's daily routine, the possibilities are endless in manifesting one's desires into reality. These two herbs work together to create a powerful energy that can support and guide individuals toward a positive and prosperous future. With the right mindset and the support of these herbs, one can truly achieve their goals and live a fulfilling life.

Mint is a potent herb that has been used for centuries to enhance one's life. Its refreshing aroma and cooling sensation have been found to awaken the senses and inspire individuals to take action toward their goals. By incorporating mint into one's daily routine, it can serve as a reminder to stay focused and motivated on the path toward success. With its energizing properties, mint can provide the necessary boost to overcome any obstacles and manifest one's desires into reality.

On the other hand, basil is a herb known for its ability to attract wealth and prosperity. It is often used in rituals and spells to bring abundance and success into one's life. Basil is also believed to have the power to protect from negative energies and promote overall well-being. When combined with mint, these two herbs create a powerful synergy that can amplify their individual properties and support individuals in their journey toward a positive and prosperous future. Together, mint and basil can guide individuals toward a fulfilling life filled with abundance and success. With the right mindset and the support of these herbs, one can overcome any challenges and manifest their desires into reality.

By incorporating these herbs into one's daily routine, they can serve as a reminder to stay focused and motivated toward achieving their goals. Trust in the power of nature and let mint and basil guide you toward a brighter and more prosperous future.

Thyme is not only a powerful herb in cooking, but it also holds great significance in the realm of manifestation. Its properties of courage, strength, and protection make it an ideal tool for those looking to manifest their desires into reality. By incorporating thyme into your daily routine, you are not only adding a delicious flavor to your meals but also a reminder to stay strong and resilient in the face of challenges. Trust in the power of thyme and let it guide you toward a brighter and more prosperous future.

In addition to thyme, mint and basil are also highly regarded for their manifestation abilities. Mint is known for its invigorating and refreshing properties, making it a great herb for boosting motivation and focus. Incorporating mint into your daily routine can serve as a gentle nudge in the right direction toward achieving your goals. Similarly, basil is believed to bring success and prosperity. By incorporating basil into your life, you are inviting abundance and prosperity into your reality. Trust in the power of nature and let these herbs guide you toward a brighter future.

Chamomile has been used for centuries as a powerful tool for promoting relaxation and emotional healing. Its gentle and soothing properties make it the perfect herb to incorporate into your daily routine. By using chamomile, you are inviting tranquility and peace into your life, allowing you to let go of stress and negative emotions. This can be especially helpful when trying to achieve your goals, as a clear and calm mind is essential for success.

In addition to its calming effects, chamomile is also associated with self-care and attracting positive energy. By taking the time to care for yourself and incorporating chamomile into your daily routine, you are sending a message to the universe that you value your well-being and are open to receiving abundance and positivity. This can be a powerful tool in manifesting your goals and desires.

Trust in the natural power of chamomile to guide you toward a brighter and more peaceful future. With its multitude of benefits, it's no wonder that chamomile has been revered by many cultures for centuries. Whether you choose to incorporate it into your daily tea, use it in aromatherapy, or even add it to your bath, chamomile is a versatile herb that can bring a sense of calm and well-being to your life. So next time you feel overwhelmed or in need of some self-care, turn to chamomile and let its gentle and soothing properties guide you toward a more peaceful and prosperous future.

Basil is a powerful herb that has been used for centuries. It is known for its strong associations with wealth, success, and abundance. This versatile herb has many benefits that can help bring positive energy into your life.

Mugwort has been used for centuries as a spiritual tool to enhance dream work and divination.

This herb is known for its gentle and soothing properties that can guide you towards a more peaceful and prosperous future. With its rich history and versatile uses, it is a valuable addition to your spiritual and practical toolkit. In addition to its spiritual benefits, Mugwort is widely used for its medicinal properties. It is believed to

have anti-inflammatory and antiseptic properties, making it a popular choice for treating skin conditions such as eczema and acne. It is also known to aid in digestion and relieve menstrual cramps. Whether you are looking to enhance your spiritual practice or improve your physical well-being, Mugwort is a powerful tool to have in your arsenal. Its ability to bring balance and clarity to your life is unparalleled. So, next time you find yourself in need of some guidance or healing, let Mugwort be your go-to herb.

Cinnamon, with its warm and spicy scent, has been used for centuries for its powerful properties. It is not only a delicious addition to culinary dishes, but it also holds a special place in spiritual practices. Its ability to attract love, passion, and prosperity is unmatched, making it a must-have for anyone looking to enhance their spiritual journey. Aside from its spiritual benefits, cinnamon is also known for its ability to support physical well-being. It is often associated with vitality and abundance, making it a popular choice for those looking to improve their overall health. Additionally, its scent has been found to have a positive effect on mood, making it a great tool for bringing balance and clarity to one's life. So, next time you find yourself in need of some guidance or healing, remember to incorporate cinnamon into your daily routine. Whether it's through burning candles or adding it to your morning coffee, this powerful herb is sure to bring positive energy and vitality to your life.

Embrace the warmth and abundance that cinnamon has to offer, and watch as it transforms your spiritual and physical well-being. Bay leaves are a powerful addition to your daily routine, providing you with protection and purification. Whether you're burning them as incense or adding them to your morning coffee, these leaves bring a warm and comforting energy to your life. They have been used for centuries in spells and rituals to manifest desires and create positive change. Embrace the abundance and vitality that bay leaves have to offer, and see how they can transform your spiritual and physical well-being. In addition to their spiritual benefits, bay leaves also have numerous physical benefits. They are known for their anti-inflammatory and anti-bacterial properties, making them a great addition to your diet. Whether consumed in tea or added to your meals, bay leaves can help boost your immune system and promote overall wellness. They are also rich in antioxidants, which can help protect your body from various diseases. By incorporating bay leaves into your daily routine, you are not only bringing positive energy into your life, but also improving your physical health.

The dandelion is revered for its many benefits, some of which include promoting overall health and well-being. It is a symbol of growth and transformation, and is often used to manifest desires and help individuals adapt to change. Its many uses make it a valuable addition to any daily routine. Dandelions are also known for their high antioxidant content, making them an excellent way to protect your body from diseases and illnesses. By incorporating dandelion into your daily life, you are not only promoting positive energy, but also boosting your physical health and strengthening your immune system. With its many uses and benefits, it is no wonder that dandelion is highly regarded in many cultures and traditions. The dandelion is not only beneficial for the body, but also for the mind and spirit. Its associations with wishes and transformation make it a powerful tool for manifestation and personal growth. By incorporating dandelion into your daily routine, you are not only taking care of your physical health, but also nurturing your spiritual and emotional well-being. Its versatility and significance in various aspects of life make it a valuable addition to any routine.

Yarrow and Dandelion are both powerful tools for manifestation and personal growth. Incorporating them into your daily routine not only takes care of your physical health, but also nurtures your spiritual and emotional well-being. Yarrow, in particular, is associated with healing, protection, and enhancing psychic abilities. It is often used for promoting physical and emotional healing, as well as providing energetic protection. Yarrow's versatility and significance in various aspects of life make it a valuable addition to any routine. It can be used in rituals, spells, and meditations to enhance intuition and psychic abilities.

Additionally, yarrow is known for its ability to purify and protect against negative energies, making it a popular choice for spiritual cleansing and protection. Its healing properties are also beneficial for those looking to overcome physical or emotional wounds and promote overall well-being. Incorporating yarrow into your daily routine can provide a deeper level of connection to the spiritual realm and enhance your overall sense of well-being. It is a versatile and powerful herb that can bring balance and healing to all aspects of life. Whether used in rituals, spells, or for physical and emotional healing, yarrow is a valuable addition to any spiritual practice or self-care routine.

Elderflower, a delicate and highly revered plant, is a powerful tool for connecting with the ancestral realm and enhancing one's overall sense of well-being. This versatile herb has been utilized in rituals, spells, and for physical and emotional healing for centuries. Its fragrant blooms bring balance and healing to all aspects of life, making it a valuable addition to any spiritual practice or self-care routine. In addition to its spiritual benefits, elderflower is also known for its medicinal properties. It has been used to treat a variety of ailments, from colds and fevers to skin irritations and digestive issues. The flower is rich in antioxidants and has anti-inflammatory properties, making it a popular choice for natural remedies. Its calming and soothing effects on the mind and body can also aid in reducing stress and anxiety, promoting a sense of peace and well-being. Elderflower's association with wisdom and guidance makes it a perfect addition to any divination practice. Its delicate blooms are said to attract the energy of the spirit realm, making it easier to connect with ancestors and receive messages from the divine. Whether used in tea, tinctures, or as an essential oil, elderflower is a versatile and powerful herb that can bring a sense of harmony and healing to all who seek it.

Juniper is a sacred plant that has been used for centuries in spiritual practices. Its powerful and cleansing properties make it a popular choice for banishing negative energies and promoting purification. In the spirit realm, juniper is known for its ability to ward off harmful influences and protect those who seek its guidance. In ancient times, juniper was considered a sacred herb that connected humans to the divine. It was believed that burning juniper incense would help individuals communicate with their ancestors and receive messages from the spirit realm. Its strong scent was thought to open up channels of communication, making it easier for the spirit to connect with the physical world. For this reason, juniper was highly valued and often used in ceremonies and rituals. Today, juniper is still highly regarded for its spiritual properties. It is often used in tea, tinctures, or as an essential oil to bring a sense of harmony and healing to those who seek it. Juniper is a versatile herb that can be used in various forms, making it easily accessible for spiritual practices. Its energy is strong and pure, making it a powerful tool for connecting with the spirit realm and receiving guidance from the divine.

Juniper is not the only herb with powerful spiritual properties. Patchouli, for example, has its own unique abilities that make it a valuable tool for spiritual growth and healing. This earthy, grounding herb is often used for attracting abundance and prosperity, making it a favorite among those seeking financial success. Its fertility and attraction properties also lend themselves well to rituals focused on sensuality, allowing individuals to connect with their own desires and manifest them into reality. In addition to its powerful energetic properties, patchouli is also known for its versatility. This herb can be used in various forms, such as essential oils, dried leaves, and incense, making it easily accessible for any spiritual practice. Its soothing and calming scent is ideal for meditation, helping individuals to connect with their inner selves and the divine. It is also commonly used in spell work, adding an extra boost of energy and intention to any ritual. For those seeking guidance from the spiritual realm, patchouli is a valuable tool. Its grounding properties help individuals to remain centered and focused, while its attraction abilities help to draw in messages and guidance from the divine. Whether used alone or in combination with other herbs, patchouli is a powerful tool for anyone on a spiritual journey of growth and healing.

Herbs have been used in witchcraft for centuries, and their properties and associations are still being discovered and utilized today. Each herb has its own unique energy and purpose, making them essential tools for any practitioner. Understanding the history and potential effects of herbs is crucial in incorporating them into magical practice, and ethical harvesting practices are a must to maintain respect for the natural world. As with any tool, intention and respect are key in harnessing the full power of herbs in witchcraft. Patchouli, in particular, is a revered herb in the spiritual community, known for its grounding and attraction properties. It has been used for centuries in ceremonies and rituals, aiding individuals in staying centered and focused. Its ability to attract messages and guidance from the divine makes it a powerful tool for those on a spiritual journey of growth and healing. Whether used alone or in combination with other herbs, patchouli can amplify and enhance the intentions of any magical practice. Working with herbs in witchcraft is a powerful way to connect with nature and harness its energies for spiritual growth and healing. Each herb has its unique qualities and associations, making it essential to do research and understand their properties before incorporating them into magical practice. By respecting the natural world and using ethical harvesting practices, witches can honor the earth and its gifts while utilizing the full power of herbs in their craft.

Chapter 11

An Introduction to Runes

In ancient times, Germanic and Nordic tribes used runes as a form of writing, divination, and magic. These symbols were believed to hold great power and were used for various purposes, including gaining insight, protection, and manifesting positive intentions.

Today, runes are still used in white witchcraft as a tool for practicing magic and connecting with the spiritual realm. For those who practice white magic, runes are an essential part of their craft.

These symbols are believed to have their own unique energy and meanings, making them powerful tools for manifestation and spiritual guidance. By tapping into the energy of the runes, practitioners can strengthen their intentions and bring positivity into their lives. Using runes in white magic involves more than just writing or drawing them. It requires a deep understanding of their meanings and how to interpret them in different situations. Each rune has its own significance and can be used in various ways to achieve different goals. With proper knowledge and guidance, one can harness the power of runes to enhance their magical practice and invite positivity into their lives.

Runes have a rich and extensive history, with origins dating back to the 2nd century AD. The most well-known runes are from the Elder Futhark, the oldest form of the runic alphabet with 24 symbols. These symbols were used by Germanic peoples for writing, divination, and magical purposes. Each rune has its own unique origin and significance, with some representing deities or natural elements, while others hold more abstract meanings. As the runic alphabet evolved and spread, different cultures and traditions adopted their own variations of the symbols. This diversity adds depth and complexity to the interpretation and use of runes in different situations.

Studying the origins and history of runes can help deepen your understanding and connection to their use. By learning about their cultural context and evolution, you can gain a greater appreciation for the power and significance of each rune. This knowledge can also provide insight into how runes were used in the past and how they can be applied in modern magical practice.

Runes were used in divination and magic rituals, providing insight and guidance to those who sought it. Each rune was believed to be connected to a specific deity or force, adding a spiritual element to their use. The runic alphabet was not only a means of communication but also a tool for invoking the power and energy of the divine. Learning about the cultural context and evolution of runes can deepen your understanding and respect for these ancient symbols. It can also reveal the ways in which runes were utilized in the past, from casting lots to carving them into objects for protection or good luck.

By understanding the origins of runes, one can better appreciate their significance and purpose. In modern magical practice, runes can still be used for divination and spellwork. By combining the traditional meanings with one's own intuition, runes can provide guidance and insight into current situations. This ancient form of magic continues to be relevant and powerful, connecting us to our past and allowing us to tap into the energy of the universe. By expanding our knowledge of runes, we can expand our understanding of the world around us.

Casting runes is not only a mystical practice but also a way to gain insight into our current situations. As we delve into this ancient form of magic, we are able to connect with our past and tap into the energy of the universe. By expanding our knowledge of runes, we can expand our understanding of the world around us. This expansion allows us to gain a deeper understanding of the meanings and interpretations of the runes, providing us with even more guidance and insight.

During a rune casting, the placement of the runes is crucial. Each rune has a specific meaning, and when drawn, it can provide valuable information and guidance. The position of the runes can also add to the overall interpretation, making each reading unique and personalized. Whether the runes land upright, reversed, or overlap, each position adds to the nuance of the reading, giving us a more complete picture of the situation at hand. This makes rune casting a powerful tool for answering specific questions or providing general guidance in our lives. As we continue to expand our understanding of runes, we open ourselves up to a world of knowledge and wisdom. By tapping into this ancient form of magic, we are able to gain valuable insights and guidance into our lives. Runes have stood the test of time and continue to be relevant and powerful, connecting us to our past and allowing us to tap into the energy of the universe. With each rune casting, we gain a deeper understanding of ourselves and the world around us, making us more connected and in tune with the universe.

The process of creating runes is a sacred one, with practitioners pouring their own energy and intention into each individual symbol. Whether carved from wood, etched onto stones, or crafted from bones, each set is unique and holds a special connection to its creator. The red markings on the runes are believed to hold strong power in spellwork, symbolizing life and vitality. The act of creating runes is not simply a physical task but a spiritual one as well. The runes are imbued with the energy of the universe, connecting us to our past and allowing us to tap into the powerful forces that surround us. As we carve each symbol and infuse it with our own energy, we are simultaneously gaining a deeper understanding of ourselves and the world around us. This connection to the universe makes us more in tune with the energies and forces at play, allowing us to harness their power for our own growth and spiritual development.

Integrating with spellwork allows us to tap into the powerful energies of the universe to enhance our magical practices. By using runes, we can amplify the intentions of our spells and manifest our desires more effectively. By carefully selecting the appropriate runes for a specific spell, we can channel the energies of each symbol and align them with our intentions. Through the use of runes in spellwork, we are able to form a deeper connection with the natural world and the energies that flow through it. This connection allows us to not only gain a better understanding of ourselves but also of the world around us. As we become more attuned to the energies at play, we are better equipped to utilize them for our own growth and spiritual development. This integration of runes with spellwork creates a powerful synergy that can bring about profound and transformative results. The practice of utilizing runes in spellwork is not only a way to manifest our intentions but also a way to deepen our understanding of the world around us. As we become more attuned to the energies at play, we begin to realize the power and influence they have on our lives. This realization can lead to a greater sense of control and agency in our own spiritual development.

One of the most intriguing aspects of integrating runes with spellwork is the powerful synergy that is created. When used together, these two practices can amplify the effects of each other, resulting in profound and transformative results. The use of runes in spellwork can lend a sense of ancient wisdom and tradition to our modern witchcraft practices, connecting us to our ancestral roots and invoking a deeper sense of magic.

One of the most useful ways to utilize runes in spellwork is for protection and binding. Runes such as 'Algiz' can be used to create boundaries or safeguard spaces, making them a valuable tool for those who feel the need to protect themselves or their loved ones. These runes are often included in protective amulets or used in rituals that shield against negative energies. By incorporating runes into our spellwork, we can tap into their powerful protective properties and harness their energy to create a safe and secure environment for ourselves and others.

Runes have been used for centuries as a form of divination and a means of communication with the divine. However, it is important to acknowledge the ethical considerations that come with incorporating them into our spellwork. As with any form of magic, the intent behind the use of runes is crucial. It is imperative that we approach them with respect and clarity, ensuring that our actions align with the fundamental principle of causing no harm. As practitioners of white witchcraft, we must remember to always use our powers for the greater good. This includes being mindful of the intentions we set when working with runes. Before casting any spells, it is important to reflect on our motivations and ensure that they align with our values and beliefs. By doing so, we can ensure that our use of runes is not only effective but also in line with our ethical code.

Incorporating runes into our magical practices can be a powerful tool for protection and warding off negative energies. However, as with any form of magic, it is crucial that we use them responsibly and ethically. By doing so, we can tap into the full potential of these ancient symbols and create a safe and harmonious environment for ourselves and our loved ones.

Fehu (F) is a powerful rune that symbolizes wealth, abundance, and prosperity. In ancient times, it was often used to represent livestock, which was a valuable source of wealth for many communities. Today, Fehu is still a potent symbol of material gain and possession, but it also carries a deeper meaning of responsibility. It reminds us that with wealth comes great responsibility, and we must use it wisely and ethically. As with all forms of magic, it is crucial that we use Fehu responsibly and with good intentions. It is not a tool to be used for selfish gain or to harm others. Instead, it should be used to create a safe and harmonious environment for ourselves and our loved ones. When we tap into the power of Fehu, we can attract abundance and prosperity into our lives, while warding off negative energies that may disrupt our peace and well-being. However, we must also be mindful of the potential negative consequences of using Fehu irresponsibly. Just as with any form of magic, there is always a risk of backfiring or causing harm if we are not careful.

This is why it is essential to approach Fehu with respect and caution, and to always keep in mind the ethical implications of our actions. By using Fehu responsibly, we can unlock its full potential and create a more prosperous and fulfilling life for ourselves and those around us. Uruz (U) and Fehu are both powerful symbols in Norse mythology, representing wealth and strength respectively. However, with great power comes great responsibility. We must approach these symbols with caution and respect, keeping in mind the ethical implications of our actions. This means using them responsibly and not allowing our desires to cloud our judgment. By doing so, we can unlock their full potential and create a more prosperous and fulfilling life for ourselves and those around us.

Uruz, in particular, symbolizes strength, health, and vitality. It is often associated with the wild ox, representing raw, untamed energy that can be harnessed for the individual's growth and health. This energy can be a double-edged sword, as it can be both a source of great strength and a destructive force if not kept in check. It is important to approach this energy with mindfulness and discipline, using it for our own personal growth and well-being, rather than allowing it to control us. With this approach, we can harness the power of Uruz to become stronger and healthier individuals, both physically and mentally. Thurisaz (Þ) is a powerful symbol that has been associated with the Norse god Thor and his mighty hammer. It represents strength, defense, and protection, but it also has a deeper meaning. This rune can also symbolize a challenge or obstacle that must be overcome in order to reach our goals. Just like Thor used his hammer to protect and defend his people, we too can use the energy of Thurisaz to confront and overcome any challenges that come our way. However, it is important to approach this energy with mindfulness and discipline. We must not let the power of Thurisaz control us, but instead use it for our own personal growth and well-being. By doing so, we can harness its strength and become stronger and healthier individuals, both physically and mentally. This rune teaches us that challenges are a natural part of life, and it is how we face them that truly matters. With the help of Thurisaz, we can learn to embrace challenges and use them as opportunities for growth and development.

In Norse mythology, Thor used his hammer to protect his people and fight against evil forces. Similarly, Thurisaz reminds us to be brave and stand up for what we believe in. It encourages us to face our fears head-on and overcome them with strength and determination. By facing our challenges with the energy of Thurisaz, we can emerge as victorious and powerful individuals, ready to take on whatever life throws our way. So let us embrace the power of Thurisaz and use it to become the best versions of ourselves. Ansuz, also known as (A), is a powerful rune associated with Odin, the leader of the Aesir, the Norse gods. This rune symbolizes wisdom and communication, making it a potent tool for those seeking guidance and knowledge. With Ansuz on our side, we can tap into the wisdom of the gods and receive their messages and guidance. Moreover, Ansuz is also connected with leadership and authority figures. This rune reminds us to trust our own inner wisdom and take charge of our lives. We have the power to be our own leaders and make decisions with confidence and clarity, just like Odin, the ruler of the gods. By embracing the energy of Ansuz, we can step into our own power and become leaders in our own right. Let us remember the power of Ansuz and the wisdom and leadership it represents. With this rune by our side, we can communicate effectively, receive guidance from the gods, and become the leaders of our own lives. So let us embrace Ansuz and its powerful energy, and use it to guide us on our journey to becoming the best versions of ourselves.

Let us embrace Raidho (R) and its energy of travel and rhythm, and use it to guide us towards our goals. As we embark on our journey, we must remember that the right action at the right time is essential. The journey can be challenging, but with the guidance of Raidho, we can navigate through the twists and turns, and reach our destination with confidence and determination. Together, Ansuz and Raidho remind us that effective communication is key in becoming the leaders of our own lives. With these runes, we can find our voice, share our knowledge and wisdom, and inspire others to do the same. Let us embrace these powerful energies, and trust in their ability to guide us towards becoming the best versions of ourselves. Kenaz (K), also known as the rune of torch and light, represents a powerful symbol of enlightenment and knowledge. Just like a torch illuminates the path in the dark, Kenaz guides us towards a greater understanding of our own lives. It inspires us to seek out knowledge and learn from our experiences, allowing us to grow and evolve into the best versions of ourselves. Moreover, Kenaz is also associated with creativity and the flame of inspiration. It encourages us to tap into our inner creativity and use it to express ourselves and share our unique perspectives with the world. With Kenaz, we are reminded that we all have a unique light within us, and it is our responsibility to let it shine and inspire others to do the same. Through the powerful energies of Kenaz, we are encouraged to embrace our own voice and trust in our abilities. It reminds us that we are the leaders of our own lives, and we have the power to shape our destiny. By following the guidance of Kenaz, we can find our own unique path and inspire others to do the same. Let us welcome the light of Kenaz into our lives and trust in its ability to guide us towards becoming the best versions of ourselves.

Gebo (G), or the rune of generosity and balance, reminds us of the importance of giving and receiving in our relationships. It symbolizes the idea that when we offer gifts or acts of kindness to others, we not only bring them closer to us but also create a sense of balance and harmony between us. This rune encourages us to be open and giving, knowing that this will ultimately lead to stronger and more meaningful connections with those around us. In addition to representing generosity, Gebo also reminds us of the importance of reciprocity. It encourages us to not only give freely, but also to be open to receiving with gratitude. By embracing this balance of giving and receiving, we can create a continuous flow of positive energy in our relationships and in our lives. Gebo reminds us that true balance is achieved when we are both givers and receivers, and that both are necessary for the health of our connections with others. Let us embrace the energy of Gebo and strive to create more balance and generosity in our relationships. By giving freely and being open to receiving, we can strengthen our connections and bring more harmony and fulfillment into our lives. As we move forward, let us remember the lesson of this rune and strive to embody its spirit of generosity and balance in all aspects of our lives. By embracing the spirit of giving and openness, we can cultivate a more harmonious and fulfilling existence.

As we strive to embody the qualities of Wunjo (W), we align ourselves with the energy of joy, comfort, and pleasure. This rune reminds us that true happiness comes from within and through our connections with others. When we approach life with a spirit of generosity and balance, we create an atmosphere of abundance and ease. This attracts positive relationships and opportunities, bringing more harmony and fulfillment into our lives. Let us remember this lesson and spread joy and kindness wherever we go, knowing that we are capable of creating our own happiness. Let us also strive to bring balance and harmony to all aspects of our lives. This includes finding a balance between giving and receiving, as well as nurturing our own well-being. By taking care of ourselves, we are better able to show up for others and create strong and prosperous relationships. With Wunjo as our guide, we can create a life filled with joy, comfort, and abundance.

Hagalaz (H) reminds us that even though destruction can be painful, it can also bring about new beginnings and growth. Just like a hailstorm may damage crops, it also nourishes the soil and prepares it for a new season of growth. This rune teaches us the importance of embracing change and seeing the potential for growth and transformation in every situation. By letting go of what no longer serves us, we make space for new opportunities and experiences to come into our lives. In this way, Hagalaz is a reminder that balance is necessary for our personal well-being and growth. We cannot always control external forces, but we can choose how we respond to them. By taking care of ourselves and finding inner peace and strength, we are better equipped to handle challenges and support those around us. Hagalaz encourages us to find a balance between giving and receiving, nurturing ourselves and others, and embracing both destruction and growth in our lives.

Let Hagalaz be our guide as we navigate life's storms and find the silver lining in every cloud. By embracing the cycles of destruction and growth, we can create a life filled with joy, comfort, and abundance. Just as the hailstorm rejuvenates the soil, let us allow the challenges we face to nourish our souls and lead us toward our highest potential. With Hagalaz by our side, we can weather any storm and emerge stronger and more resilient than before.

Nauthiz (N) teaches us that we must embrace our struggles and use them as stepping stones toward self-growth. Just as the hailstorm rejuvenates the soil, the challenges we face nourish our souls and lead us toward our highest potential. It is through these hardships that we learn to endure and become stronger individuals. With Nauthiz by our side, we are reminded that our struggles serve a purpose in our journey toward self-discovery. They allow us to reflect on ourselves and our priorities, and to make necessary changes for our personal growth. This rune encourages us to push through the tough times, knowing that they will ultimately lead us to a place of joy, comfort, and abundance. Nauthiz reminds us that our journey toward self-growth is not meant to be easy, but it is necessary for our personal development. It is through overcoming challenges and enduring hardships that we truly find our strength and resilience. Just as the hailstorm nourishes the soil, our struggles nourish our souls and prepare us for the abundance that awaits us. Let us embrace the lessons that Nauthiz teaches us and continue to weather any storm that comes our way.

In Norse mythology, the rune Isa (I) represents ice, which can symbolize a period of stillness or a lack of change. Just as ice remains frozen and unmoving, Isa may suggest that it is a time for us to pause and reflect. It reminds us that sometimes progress must be halted in order for us to gain clarity and direction. Isa also serves as a reminder that hardships and struggles are a necessary part of our journey. Just as the hailstorm nourishes the soil, our struggles nourish our souls and help us grow stronger. They teach us valuable lessons and prepare us for the abundance that awaits us in the future. In this way, Isa serves as a reminder to embrace our struggles and use them as opportunities for growth and self-discovery. As we weather any storm that comes our way, we become more resilient and better equipped to handle any challenges that may come our way in the future. As we continue on our journey, let us keep the lessons of Isa and Nauthiz in mind. Let us embrace the stillness and pause when needed, and use our struggles as opportunities to nourish our souls and grow stronger. By doing so, we can weather any storm that comes our way and emerge even stronger and more resilient than before. So let us welcome the lessons of Isa and trust that they will lead us toward abundance and growth.

Jera (J) is a powerful rune that reminds us that our hard work and patience will eventually pay off. It represents the bountiful harvest that we reap when we stay committed to our goals and put in the effort. As we welcome the lessons of Isa and trust that they will lead us toward abundance and growth, we must also recognize that Jera is a symbol of reaping the rewards of our efforts. Patience is key when working toward our goals, and Jera reminds us that good things come to those who wait. This rune teaches us to trust in the process, even when things seem difficult or slow. By nourishing our souls and growing stronger through these challenges, we can weather any storm that comes our way and emerge even more resilient than before. Jera is a reminder that our patience and hard work will bring us the rewards we deserve.

Eihwaz (E) is a powerful symbol of resilience and perseverance. Just like the yew tree, we must have the endurance and strength to withstand the challenges that come our way. This rune teaches us that no matter how difficult or slow our progress may seem, we must keep pushing forward with determination. By doing so, we can emerge even stronger and more resilient than before. Eihwaz (E) reminds us that true strength lies in our ability to endure and overcome obstacles. It encourages us to tap into our inner will to survive and to keep moving forward, no matter how daunting the journey may seem. This rune teaches us that with patience and hard work, we can weather any storm and ultimately reap the rewards we deserve. It serves as a powerful reminder that our struggles are not in vain and that they are ultimately shaping us into stronger, more resilient beings.

Expanding on the previous context, Perthro (P) is a rune that delves into the mysteries of fate and the power of the unknown. In Norse mythology, this rune is closely linked to the Norns, the powerful goddesses who control the destinies of gods and men alike. It serves as a reminder that our paths are often determined by forces beyond our control, and that we must embrace the uncertainty of life. However, Perthro is not just about destiny and the unknown. It also carries connotations of play and chance. This rune reminds us to take risks and embrace the unexpected. Life is full of surprises, and it is through taking chances that we can truly grow and evolve. By embracing the playful and unpredictable aspects of life, we can open ourselves up to new opportunities and experiences. In essence, Perthro is a powerful reminder that life is a journey full of twists and turns. It teaches us to have faith in the unknown and to trust that our struggles will ultimately lead us to where we need to be. With patience, hard work, and a willingness to take chances, we can weather any storm and emerge stronger and more resilient than ever before. So embrace the mystery of fate, and let Perthro guide you toward your ultimate destiny.

Algiz (Z) is a powerful symbol of protection, a guardian that shields us from danger and harm. The splayed fingers evoke a sense of warding, as if creating a barrier between us and the forces that threaten us. In the face of adversity, Algiz stands as a beacon of safety and reassurance, reminding us that we are not alone and that we are always protected. This rune is also often associated with the divine, suggesting that we are under the watchful eye of a higher power, guiding and protecting us on our journey. As we embrace the mystery of fate and let Perthro guide us toward our ultimate destiny, we can also call upon the strength and protection of Algiz. With patience, hard work, and a willingness to take chances, we can weather any storm that comes our way and emerge even stronger and more resilient. Like a shield, Algiz offers us a sense of security and stability, allowing us to move forward with confidence and courage. Let this powerful symbol be our guide as we navigate through life's challenges and obstacles, knowing that we are always protected and defended. Algiz, the rune of protection and defense, allows us to move forward with confidence and courage. Just like a shield, it offers us a sense of security and stability, making us even stronger and more resilient. When facing life's challenges and obstacles, we can always turn to Algiz for guidance and protection. It serves as a reminder that we are not alone in our journey and that we will always find a way to overcome any difficulties that come our way.

Sowilo (S), on the other hand, represents the sun, the ultimate symbol of success and energy. It reminds us that no matter how dark our path may seem, there will always be a glimmer of hope and light to guide us toward positive outcomes. Just like the sun gives life to all living beings, Sowilo brings us solace and the promise of a brighter tomorrow. It serves as a beacon of hope, reminding us to never lose faith and to always keep moving forward. Together, Algiz and Sowilo offer a powerful combination of strength, protection, and hope. They guide us through life's journey, helping us to overcome any challenges that come our way. With these powerful symbols by our side, we can face each day with confidence and courage, knowing that we are always protected and defended. May Algiz and Sowilo be our guiding light, reminding us to always stay strong and never lose hope.

Tiwaz (T) is a powerful symbol that reminds us to always strive for victory and justice, even in the face of challenges. It represents strong leadership and the need for balance in all aspects of life. Just like Tyr, the

A Baby Witches Guide To Greatness

Norse god it is named after, Tiwaz teaches us the value of sacrifice for the greater good. With Tiwaz by our side, we can overcome any obstacle and achieve success with integrity and honor.

Ehwaz (E) is a rune that symbolizes trust, teamwork, and progress. It reminds us that we are not alone and that we can achieve more when we work together. Like two horses pulling a chariot, Ehwaz teaches us the importance of cooperation and communication in order to move forward and make progress. With Ehwaz as our guide, we can trust in our abilities and those of others, knowing that together, we can overcome any challenge that comes our way. With Tiwaz and Ehwaz as our guiding lights, we can face each day with confidence and courage, knowing that we are always protected and defended. These powerful symbols serve as reminders to always stay strong and never lose hope, no matter what obstacles may come our way. They represent the strength and resilience within each of us, and with their guidance, we can navigate through life's challenges and emerge victorious. Let us embrace these symbols and their meanings, and allow them to guide us toward a brighter and more fulfilling future.

Berkana (B) is a powerful symbol that reminds us of our inner strength and resilience. Like the birch tree, we are capable of growth and renewal, even in the face of adversity. This feminine energy guides us toward new beginnings and empowers us to birth new ideas. Let us embrace the birch tree and its message of hope and transformation. Additionally, the symbol of Berkana (B) may also represent the importance of motherhood and the nurturing energy of the feminine. Just as the birch tree provides shelter and nourishment to its young, so too do mothers provide love and support to their children. Through this connection, we can find comfort and guidance as we navigate through life's obstacles. Let us honor and celebrate the strength and resilience of mothers and all those who embody the spirit of Berkana (B).

Mothers embody the spirit of Berkana (B), providing love and support to their young children. This connection provides comfort and guidance as we navigate through the obstacles of life. The strength and resilience of mothers are to be honored and celebrated. The Mannaz (M) symbolizes the self and humanity, reflecting on human relationships and the individual's role within society. It is a reminder that we are all interconnected and that our actions can impact those around us. The love and support provided by mothers is a perfect example of the human connection and the role of individuals in society. It is a reminder to be kind and compassionate toward others, just as mothers are toward their children. The Mannaz (M) symbol also serves as a reminder to appreciate the sacrifices that mothers make for their children and the love that they give unconditionally. It encourages us to acknowledge and celebrate the strength and resilience of mothers and all those who embody the spirit of Berkana (B). Let us remember to show our gratitude and appreciation for the selfless acts of mothers and the important role they play in society.

Laguz (L), on the other hand, represents the flow and journey of life, much like water. It is a symbol of the subconscious and intuition, urging us to dive deep into our minds and emotions. It reminds us to listen to our inner voice and trust our instincts, for they are powerful tools for self-discovery and growth. Laguz also suggests a need for reflection and contemplation, as we navigate the constantly changing currents of life. Together, Berkana and Laguz remind us to honor and celebrate the strength and resilience of mothers, who embody the spirit of both symbols. They also encourage us to tap into our own inner strength and intuition, as we navigate the ebbs and flows of life. Let us not forget to show our appreciation for the selfless acts of mothers and embrace the journey of self-discovery and growth that Laguz represents.

Ingwaz (NG) is a powerful symbol in Norse mythology and represents the potential within all of us. It is said to be connected to the male fertility god Ing, who is associated with abundance and growth. This rune reminds us that we have the ability to create and manifest our desires, but it also reminds us that growth takes time and effort. Just as a seed needs to be nurtured and cared for in order to grow, so do our own goals and dreams. In addition to potential and growth, Ingwaz also speaks to the importance of internal work and reflection. It is a rune of gestation, representing the unseen work that happens behind the scenes before we see tangible results. This is a reminder to trust in the process and have faith in our own inner strength and intuition. Just as a mother carries and nurtures a child before giving birth, we too must nurture and care for our own dreams and goals before they can come to fruition. As we navigate the ebbs and flows of life, let us not forget to show our appreciation for the selfless acts of mothers. They are a true embodiment of the power and potential of Ingwaz, constantly nurturing and growing their children with unconditional love. And as we embrace the journey of self-discovery and growth that Laguz represents, let us remember that we are all capable of tapping into our own inner strength and potential, just like the male fertility god Ing.

As we continue to delve into the world of Norse mythology, we come across the rune Dagaz (D). This rune represents the transition from darkness to light, from ignorance to knowledge. It is a symbol of new beginnings and the promise of a brighter future ahead. Dagaz serves as a reminder that even in the darkest of times, there is always the potential for growth and transformation. Just like the male fertility god Ing, we are constantly evolving and nurturing our own inner potential. When we tap into our own inner strength, we are capable of achieving great things and breaking through any barriers that stand in our way. So let us embrace the journey of self-discovery and growth, just like the constant nurturing and unconditional love of Ingwaz. And as we move forward, let us remember that the rune Laguz represents the ever-flowing waters of life, and it is through this journey that we can fully tap into our own potential and awaken our true selves. Let the light of Dagaz guide us toward our own breakthroughs and awakenings, and may we always find clarity and relief in the face of challenges and difficult periods.

In the journey towards discovering our true selves and unlocking our full potential, Othala serves as a guide. It represents not only our heritage and home, but also our inheritance – both tangible and intangible. Our ancestral land and spiritual legacy are important facets of who we are and help shape our identity. Through Othala (O), we can connect with our roots and find a sense of belonging. In challenging times, Othala reminds us of what truly matters. It encourages us to seek clarity and relief and to look to our heritage and home for strength and guidance. Our ancestors have faced their own struggles and have passed down their wisdom and resilience to us. With the light of Dagaz and the support of our heritage, we can navigate through difficult periods and emerge stronger and more enlightened. As we continue on our journey, may we always remember the significance of Othala. It is a reminder to embrace our heritage and home and to honor our inheritance. Through this, we can gain a deeper understanding of ourselves and our place in the world. Let Othala be our constant companion as we tap into our potential and awaken our true selves. Remember, meanings can vary according to different interpretations and contexts.

Traditionally, runes were much more than an alphabet; they were seen as holding magical properties and were used for various forms of divination and invoking deities. The study and interpretation of runes is a never-ending journey of learning and intuition. Each rune has its own unique energy and meaning, which can be influenced by the individual using them. Through journaling and reflection, one can tap into their own inner wisdom and uncover the personal significance of each rune. In the practice of white witchcraft, runes are not just a simple alphabet but hold powerful magical properties. They are used for divination, connecting with higher powers, and manifesting intentions. Through comprehensive study and meditation, one can deepen their understanding of the runes and harness their full potential as a tool for personal growth and transformation. The more we work with runes, the more we awaken our true selves and unlock our innate abilities to manifest our desires. As we tap into the energy of the runes, we strengthen our intuition and develop a deeper connection with the universe. It is a constant companion on our journey toward self-discovery and empowerment. Remember, the meanings of runes can vary and evolve as we continue to explore their depths on our path to enlightenment.

Chapter 12
Basic spell work for beginners

Here are ten essential beginner-friendly spells that can be used in both white and green witchcraft, helping you tap into natural energies and enhance your practice.

Protection

This spell is perfect for those looking to add a layer of protection to their everyday life. It's a great beginner spell because it utilizes simple materials that can easily be found in any witch's pantry. The small white candle represents purity and light, while the rosemary or sage and salt both hold powerful cleansing properties. The clear quartz crystal is known for its ability to amplify energy and intention, making it the perfect tool for this spell. To begin, create a sacred space by lighting the candle and sprinkling salt around it in a circle. This will help to create a safe and protected area for you to work in. As you hold the quartz crystal in your hand, take a moment to visualize a protective barrier forming around you. This could be in the form of a bubble or a shield, whichever feels most comfortable to you. Next, gently pass the crystal through the flame of the candle. This will imbue it with the energy of the candle, adding an extra boost to your spell. Then, hold the crystal over the smoke of the burning herb, allowing it to absorb the cleansing properties. While doing so, recite a simple protection chant or affirmation. This could be something as simple as "I am safe and protected at all times" or "I am surrounded by a barrier of light and love." Finally, carry the crystal with you or place it near your bed to continue the protective energy throughout your day and night.

Healing

Release the negative energy and replace it with positive healing energy by performing this simple and powerful healing spell. The materials needed are easily accessible and the instructions are simple to follow. Begin by lighting a candle and filling a small bowl with fresh or dried lavender. As you sit in front of the candle, take a few deep breaths and focus on the person or situation you wish to heal. Visualize the healing energy flowing from the candle into the lavender, filling it with powerful healing properties. Take your time and allow yourself to fully immerse in the healing energy as you meditate. Once you feel ready, blow out the candle and place the bowl of lavender in a prominent place in your home. The healing energy will continue to radiate, creating a calming and positive atmosphere. This spell can be performed whenever you feel the need to release any negative energy and replace it with healing energy. It can also be used to bring peace and harmony to any situation or relationship in need of healing. In addition to performing this spell, you can also enhance its effects by carrying a crystal with you or placing it near your bed. The crystal will continue to emit protective and healing energy throughout your day and night. Use this spell as a daily ritual to promote overall well-being and positivity in your life. Remember, the power of healing lies within you, and this simple spell can help you tap into that power and manifest it into your life.

Attraction Spell

Harness the powerful energy of nature to attract positivity and well-being into your life. This daily ritual allows you to tap into your own healing abilities and manifest your desires. The Attraction Spell is a simple yet effective way to bring more abundance and happiness into your life. To begin, gather your materials and set aside a few minutes each day to perform the spell. As you plant the basil seeds and water them, focus on the qualities and experiences you wish to attract. Visualize the seeds growing into healthy plants, symbolizing the growth and manifestation of your desires. With each day, tend to the plants and nurture your intentions as the basil flourishes. Just as the plants grow and thrive, so too will your desires come to fruition. Trust in the power of this spell and the universe to bring you all that you desire. Remember, the power of attraction lies within you, and this simple spell is just a tool to help you harness it.

Prosperity Spell

As the green candle flickers, its flame dancing to the rhythm of your heart, envision your goals coming to life. The warmth of the cinnamon permeates the room, filling it with the comforting scent of abundance. With each breath, you feel the universe responding to your intentions, aligning itself to bring your desires to fruition. As you hold the citrine crystal, its vibrant energy radiates through your fingertips, connecting you to the spell and amplifying your intentions. You can feel the power building within you, igniting a sense of confidence and trust in the universe. With each pass through the candle flame, the crystal absorbs the energy and releases it back into your hands, a constant cycle of manifestation. This spell is a reminder that the power of attraction lies within you. The combination of the green candle, cinnamon, and citrine crystal is simply a tool to help you harness that power and manifest your desires. As you continue to trust in the process and stay aligned with your intentions, the universe will respond in kind, bringing you all that you desire and more. So take a deep breath, release any doubts, and trust in the power of this prosperity spell to bring abundance into your life.

Cleansing Spell

When it comes to manifesting abundance and prosperity in our lives, it is important to trust in the process and stay aligned with our intentions. The universe is always responding to our energy and thoughts, and when we approach a prosperity spell with doubt and fear, we may unintentionally block the flow of abundance. So, take a deep breath and release any doubts, knowing that the power of this cleansing spell will bring clarity and purity into your life. To fully cleanse our energy and space, we must gather the necessary materials and follow the instructions carefully. The white sage bundle serves as a powerful tool for clearing negative energy, and the abalone shell or fireproof dish provides a safe space to catch the ashes. As we light the sage and allow it to smolder, we are creating a cleansing smoke that will help release any stagnant energy and replace it with a sense of clarity and purity. Using the feather to waft the smoke around ourselves or throughout our living space allows for a thorough cleanse, as we visualize the negative energy dissipating. Once the cleansing is complete, it is important to extinguish the sage in the shell or dish and open windows to let fresh air in. This symbolizes the release of any negative energy and the welcoming of new, positive energy. Trust in the power of this prosperity spell and know that by taking the time to cleanse our energy and space, we are opening ourselves up to receive all that we desire and more. Remember to approach this spell with intention and trust in the process, and the universe will respond in kind.

Love Spell

By cleansing our energy and space, we are creating a space for love to enter and manifest in our lives. The pink candle represents love, the rose petals symbolize beauty and romance, and the rose quartz crystal embodies unconditional love and healing. As we light the candle, we are igniting our intentions and inviting love into our lives. The crystal, passed through the candle flame, is charged with the energy of love and becomes a powerful tool in our manifestation process. Keep it close to your heart, and let its energy infuse your being with love and compassion. As we visualize and focus on the love we desire, we are aligning our energy with the energy of the universe. Trust in the process and believe that love is coming your way. You can place the rose quartz on your altar as a reminder of your intention, or under your pillow to enhance the energy of love as you sleep. Remember, love is not something we can force or control, but by opening ourselves up to receiving it, we are creating space for it to naturally flow into our lives. As we continue to cleanse our energy and space, we are creating fertile ground for love to blossom and grow.

Blessing Spell

There is a powerful force of love that surrounds us, always available for us to tap into. It is not something that we can force or control, but by opening ourselves up to receiving it, we are creating space for it to naturally flow into our lives. This is where the blessing spell comes in - it acts as a powerful tool to cleanse our energy and space, allowing the flow of love and positivity to thrive. By following the instructions for the blessing spell, we are not only creating a physical representation of our intentions, but also actively infusing it with our energy and desires for blessings and positivity. As we drink the water, we are inviting the energy of blessings to flow through us, filling our space with light and harmony. This creates fertile ground for love to blossom and grow, as we continue to cleanse and open ourselves up to the abundance of love that surrounds us. The materials used in this spell - salt, lavender, and rosemary - all hold their own unique properties and energies that help to amplify the intentions of the spell. Salt is known for its purifying and cleansing properties, while lavender and rosemary are both associated with love, protection, and harmony. By combining these elements with our intentions, we are creating a powerful and intentional spell that can bring blessings and positivity into our lives. Remember to always infuse your actions with positive energy and intentions, and trust that the universe will respond in kind.

Harmony Spell

The Harmony Spell is not just a simple ritual; it is a powerful and intentional spell that combines protection, positivity, and harmony. By infusing our actions with positive energy and intentions, we attract blessings and balance into our lives. Remember to trust in the universe and its response to our intentions. To perform the Harmony Spell, you will need a blue candle and lavender oil. The blue candle symbolizes tranquility while the lavender oil promotes peace and calmness. Anoint the candle with lavender oil and light it, setting the mood for your ritual. Sit quietly and focus on cultivating peace and harmony within yourself and your surroundings. Visualize a blue light spreading around you, bringing a sense of calm and equilibrium. Once the candle has burned out, collect the remaining wax and any residual herbs and place them in a sachet or bag. This sachet will serve as a physical reminder of your intentions and can be carried with you to maintain the energy of harmony throughout your day. The Harmony Spell is a simple yet powerful way to bring balance and positivity into your life. Trust in the process and let the universe flow its blessings to you.

New Beginnings Spell

The New Beginnings Spell is a powerful tool that can help you manifest a fresh start in your life. With just a few simple materials and some focused intention, you can bring positive energy and new opportunities into your daily routine. The clear quartz crystal and white candle act as physical symbols of your desire for change and transformation. Lighting the candle and holding the crystal, you can visualize the energy of new beginnings filling your space and mind. As you pass the crystal through the flame, imagine releasing any old patterns or negative thoughts that may be holding you back. Focus on the feeling of lightness and openness that comes with letting go. Keep the crystal in a place where you will see it often, serving as a reminder of your intention for new beginnings and a symbol of the positive changes that are coming your way. Trust in the universe and allow it to flow its blessings to you. This simple spell can be carried with you throughout the day, maintaining the energy of harmony and balance in your life.

Gratitude Spell

This simple gratitude spell serves as a powerful reminder of the abundance and joy in our lives. By taking a moment to sit with a lit candle and focus on feelings of gratitude, we open ourselves up to receive even more blessings from the universe. The act of writing down the things we are grateful for amplifies this energy of abundance and allows us to fully acknowledge and appreciate the positive changes that are coming our way. Carrying this spell with us throughout the day helps us maintain the energy of harmony and balance in our lives. It serves as a symbol of our trust in the universe and its ability to flow blessings to us. By revisiting our journal or paper where we have written down our gratitude, we are reminded of the many things we have to be thankful for and can continue to attract more positivity into our lives. This gratitude spell can be a powerful tool in creating a more abundant and joyful life. By regularly practicing gratitude and acknowledging the blessings in our lives, we open ourselves up to even more blessings and positive changes. Let this spell be a daily reminder to always trust in the universe and its ability to bring goodness and abundance into our lives.

A Baby Witches Guide To Greatness

By regularly practicing gratitude and acknowledging the blessings in our lives, we open ourselves up to even more blessings and positive changes. This enables us to cultivate a more positive and joyful life, filled with abundance and goodness. As we trust in the universe and its ability to bring positivity into our lives, we are able to manifest our desires and intentions with more ease and clarity. These beginner spells provide a foundation for incorporating white and green witchcraft into your practice and can be adapted to suit your personal intentions and spiritual path. They serve as a daily reminder to always trust in the universe and its ability to bring goodness and abundance into our lives. By incorporating these spells into our daily routine, we are able to cultivate a deeper sense of connection to the universe and the natural world around us. Remember to always practice spells with respect for free will and ethical considerations, and to approach magic with a spirit of mindfulness and responsibility. These spells are not meant to control or manipulate others, but rather to bring positive energy and blessings into our own lives. As we continue to practice gratitude and trust in the universe, we open ourselves up to even more blessings and abundance in all aspects of our lives. Let these spells be a powerful tool in your spiritual journey towards a more joyful and fulfilling life.

~Blessed be on your magical path~

Ascher Alchier

Notes on Chapter One: Introduction
_____
_____
_____

Learning Goals:
_____
_____
_____

Notes on Chapter Two: Understanding the Basics Earth-Air-Fire-Water-Spirit-Moon-Wheel of the Year
_____
_____
_____

Learning Goals:
_____
_____
_____

Notes on Chapter Two: Notes on Earth & Grounding Work
_____
_____
_____

Learning Goals:
_____
_____
_____

Notes on Chapter Two: Deities and Air work
_____
_____
_____

A Baby Witches Guide To Greatness

Learning Goals:
_____
_____
_____

Notes on Chapter Two: Fire work
_____
_____
_____

Learning Goals:
_____
_____
_____

Notes on Chapter Two: Water Work
_____
_____
_____

Learning Goals:
_____
_____
_____

Notes on Chapter Two: Spirit Work
_____
_____
_____

Learning Goals:
_____
_____
_____

Notes on Chapter Two: Moon Work

_____
_____
_____

Learning Goals:

_____
_____
_____

Notes on Chapter Two: Year of the Wheel

_____
_____
_____

Learning Goals:

_____
_____
_____

Notes on Chapter Three: Embracing Ethics

_____
_____
_____

Learning Goals:

_____
_____
_____

Notes on Chapter Four: Spell craft ritual practice

_____
_____
_____

A Baby Witches Guide To Greatness

Learning Goals:
_____
_____
_____

Notes on Chapter Five: Connecting with divination and spirituality
_____
_____
_____

Learning Goals:
_____
_____
_____
_____

Notes on Chapter Six: Embracing natures wisdom and herbal magic
_____
_____

Learning Goals:
_____
_____
_____
_____

Notes on Chapter Seven: Living in alignment
_____
_____
_____

Learning Goals:
_____
_____
_____

Notes on Chapter Eight: Crystals
_____

Learning Goals:

Notes on Chapter Nine: Herbs

Learning Goals:

Notes on Chapter Ten: An introduction to Runes

Learning Goals:

Notes on Chapter Eleven: Basic spellwork for beginners

Learning Goals:

Rights Disclaimer:

Expansion Alchier LLC takes great pride in being the sole owner of this book, in partnership with Alchier.com. All rights are reserved, and no part of this publication can be reproduced or transmitted in any form without the prior written consent of the publisher. This includes photocopying, recording, or any other electronic or mechanical methods. However, brief quotations may be used for critical reviews and other noncommercial purposes, as permitted by copyright law. Expansion. In order to obtain permission for any use beyond the permitted brief quotations, interested parties can contact Alchier LLC through their website, www.alchier.com, or via email at Alchiershops@gmail.com. Any unauthorized use or distribution of the material in this book is strictly prohibited and may result in legal action. The publisher is dedicated to protecting their intellectual property and ensuring that their work is used in an ethical and respectful manner. Expansion. This book is a valuable resource for those interested in learning about white witchcraft, crystals, herbs, runes, and basic spell work. The learning goals for each chapter are clearly outlined, providing a roadmap for readers to expand their knowledge and understanding in these areas. Each chapter also includes notes on uses and applications, providing practical guidance for incorporating these concepts into one's practice. With this comprehensive guide, beginners can gain a solid foundation in white witchcraft and begin their journey with confidence and clarity.

Disclaimer:

This book serves as a comprehensive guide for beginners to gain a solid foundation in white witchcraft. The chapters not only provide insight into various concepts and practices but also include practical advice on how to apply them in one's own spiritual journey. The author makes it clear that the information presented is intended for educational and entertainment purposes only, and that individual beliefs and interpretations may vary. This encourages readers to explore and respect diverse perspectives and approaches to magical traditions. However, the author also emphasizes the need for caution and discretion when practicing witchcraft and magic spell work. It is important for readers to understand that these practices involve spiritual and metaphysical aspects that may not be suitable for all individuals. They are advised to consult with qualified professionals or practitioners before engaging in any form of magical or spiritual practice. The author and publisher also remind readers that they are not responsible for any consequences that may arise from the use or misuse of the information provided in this book. This serves as a reminder to readers to approach these practices with respect and responsibility.

Made in the USA
Middletown, DE
08 May 2025

75270640R00044